AWAKEN YOUR POTENTIAL

Written by

Denis Arthur Mubezi Mukalazi

Copyright © 2020

Dedication

This book is dedicated

To Israel Skyler Mubezi Nalwoga my lovely daughter who has been an inspiration throughout this process of compiling this work.

To my lovely super mother Mutawe Alice and Late Nsubuga James Takalirya my father for bringing me into this world without them I wouldn't have been.

To my special mentors and sisters Namuleme Cissy Gertrude (RIP), Nakirya Sarah and Nakibuuka Martha. These people carried the cross to ensure that I am who I am today.

Acknowledgement

Special thanks go to my entire family for supporting me and encouraging me always even in times when I've had to quarantine myself so as to concentrate on this work.

Special thanks to Nakirya Sarah, Nakibuuka Martha, Jumba Richard for their continuous support that has enabled me to have this work accomplished.

Special thanks to my siblings Lwanga Nsubuga Herbert, Katuke Noah, Kirabo Elizabeth, Nakigozi Daphne Annabel for their support.

Special thanks to all the people who knowingly or unknowingly contributed to this effort May GOD bless you all.

THANK YOU.

Preamble

Awaken your potential, the title of this book is a phrase that attracts and provokes you to realize that you have some special potential locked inside you that you ought to explore so as to get the best out of yourself. Awaken your potential further gives you an insight on how to actually spark off your real being that is unstoppable.

It is very true that every human being has a lot of potential in them but most of us hardly explore and utilize our full potential and this partly explains why some people are less progressive yet they have a lot of potential to succeed in life.

The book introduces you to the basic principles of life that you need to abreast if you are to live a successful and happy life call it stress free.

Awaken your potential has provided answers to some abstract and common riddles in life both complex and simple like What it means to know who you are; some people think that knowing your name, date of birth, clan etc. is enough to claim that you know yourself but knowing who you are is completely far from that, How your personality and mindset have affected your life, The truth about hard work and lazy ness; many people think that using too much physical energy is what makes you a hardworking person and that lazy people are those who are weak or hate to doing work but this is totally a wrong concept. This book clearly shows you what exactly qualifies someone to be hardworking and also marks out for you who exactly a lazy person is. You will be surprised.

Awakening your potential tackles the crucial aspects that contribute to people's success and failure in life to help people master the best techniques to maneuver into a permanent successful league where they are able to sustain their success and accomplished goals and also to understand how to live a better life through developing and maintaining good personality, positive thinking, positive attitude, open mindset etc.

Many people have good qualities and potential to make them the best people but having good qualities alone is not good enough what is most important is having the ability to control them that is why the author has given special attention to self-discipline and control because it is one of the most important aspects every human being needs to have but on the other hand it is what most people don't understand.

Be sure that after reading this book you will have a changed perception and attitude towards life in general, you will develop a strong mindset, Positive thinking, better knowledge of yourself in terms of potential and personality, changed attitude towards challenges, failure and own weaknesses to an extent that you will be yearning for them to come your way.

FUNDAMENTAL QUESTITIONS

1. How can you identify your personality?
2. How can you discover what you are good at?
3. How much can you achieve from the area you are good at?
4. What kind of mindset do you possess?
5. Why are you scared of pushing that idea into reality?
6. What kind of people do you need to keep around you?
7. Who deserves your precious time and how much time anyway?
8. How does response to your own failure or weaknesses impact on you?
9. Are you a hardworking person? How do account for it?
10. What exactly does the aspect of discipline mean in the world of success?
11. Why do we need challenges in life?
12. How can you become influential in life?
13. How is attitude relevant to your progress?
14. How do excuses affect your personality and success?
15. How can you improve on your personality?

NOTE

"A single chapter in a book hardly defines the entire theme though it can give an idea about the theme therefore the more chapters you open in a book the more ideas you get and the more you understand why things are represented that way which eventually helps you to dig out the main theme.

This is the same structure in life, if you open one chapter of it and stop, you will have traded your life to unalloyed failure so do not let a single chapter (failure) of your life define you forever, keep turning pages because you never know what is hidden on the next page or next chapter."

Arthur Mubezi

CHAPTER ONE
PERSONALITY

This chapter will introduce you to the aspect of personality because understanding your personality should be the first step in life when you decide to explore your full potential to succeed. Understanding your personality gives you a clear hint on what you can do best, the kind of life style you deserve, the right people to keep with, your strength and weaknesses etc.

There are various attempts defining personality from different perspectives but one thing I appreciate is that each of them agrees on some particular aspects which I summarize as;

"That mental characteristic that makes a person unique from other people in the patterns of thinking, feeling and behavior."

The main note here is that, those consistent traits a person shows at different times and in different situations in the line of thinking, feeling and behavior can determine someone's personality. In simple terms I can say that the way you think, feel and behave describes your actual personality.

> *"Personality is how you*
> *think, feel and behave at different*
> *times and in different situations"*

Arthur Mubezi

Many people never think about how their own thinking, feelings and behavior influence their lives but staying unconscious about how you think, feel and behave is a clear indication that you neither understand yourself nor know who you are. It is a very dangerous state to live a life where you don't know who you are and what you are capable of as it keeps you behind scenes of success because you'll lack a sense of direction, this is the reason why it is vital to identify and understand your personality such that you gain control over your thinking, feelings and behavior which are the primary aspects required to define your actualism. By knowing and analyzing those primary aspects of your own life, you're able to understand What you are capable of, your strength and weaknesses, interests, talents among others and it can as well help you develop and strengthen self-control which is a key pattern to success.

Our personality is built and developed right from childhood influenced by a number of things that can be categorized into three components of *Environment, Temperament* and *Character.* I will briefly explain these components because it is imperative that we understand everything right from this point so as to develop a clear picture of our own personality.

Temperament components

These are the genetically determined traits commonly known as the hereditary genes.

When we are born our minds are like a plain paper to which you can write anything however at that very moment the hereditary genes are at work defining your size, color of the skin, body formation, gender etc. As you grow up these factors become crucial and surely influence your personality in different ways. If you are short and small when you grow up, your personality is likely to be different from what it could have been if you had been tall and huge. In the same way if you had a light skin probably you would have a different personality compared to when you had pure dark skin. The same goes for gender male or female will automatically influence your personality. This influence may not seem so vivid to you but it actually influences your personality through impacting on your emotions, cognitive and behavior.

Your hereditary genes passed on by your parents or ancestors may have an impact on how other people see you or how you see yourself for example they may cause you to look at yourself as nice looking, ugly, too short, obese etc. which eventually impacts on how you perceive yourself and this will cause you to think and act in certain way acceptable or deviant.

> *"Your hereditary genes partly influence your personality but they cannot solely decree it."*

Environment components

The environment has various components that can

influence personality like places and people around us, families, friends among others. Many psychologists agree that the environment we live in combines well with the temperament factors to shape a person's personality. However, environment its self doesn't not directly impact on us but what we see, learn, live and experience in it is what shapes personality. Therefore, the consistent characteristics we show as we respond to such factors define our true personality.

"The way you perceive and respond
to environmental factors or situations around you
can determines and shape your personality."

There are some two terms that are commonly used in relation to personality development and these are **nature** and **nurture.** "*Nature*" refers to the genetic factors then "*Nurture*" refers to the environmental factors.

From a human perspective a number of credible people in this study argue and agree that high quality parenting plays a very big role in shaping our personality simply because when the parents get to understand how their children respond in certain situations they immediately begin to prepare them for such situations or even avoid exposing their children to those situations and in so doing they directly influence their children's personality.

This promotes the common saying; that good parenting produces good personalities but I personally have a divided mind on this because this will father depend on the entire surrounding. That is why we have seen cases where good parents end up with children having weird personalities like a pastor's child having a poor personality yet you would expect them to emulate their family background characterized by good character and personalities. This further explains why I say that you cannot claim to be what you are not forever such people may try to pretend when they are with their mentors but eventually their actual personality comes out.

It is the environment that gives life to other elements that put a particular impact on personality development.

Character

This is the third component which contains emotional, cognitive and behavioral patterns learned from experience which determine how someone thinks, feels and behaves.

A person's character continues to evolve throughout life though it may also depend on a person's inborn traits and early experiences.

Now that you understand the general elements that shape personality, probably you might be wondering how you can determine someone's or your own personality.

There are various ways through which someone's personality can be seen but mainly their thoughts, expression of feelings, general behavior, handling relationships and other social interactions can define it. However, the fact is that personality is unique for every person, which means that there are thousands of personalities out there in the world though there are some situations where people act in the same way in some similar situations.

Based on that fact, **David Riesman** in the early **1950s** tried to put the different personalities into specific categories hoping that these categories could help people to understand what type of personality they are, He suggested three categories of modal personalities in the world;

The ***Traditional oriented***; who emphasize doing things the way they have always been done so they hardly try out new things**,**

The ***Inner directed,*** who are always guilty oriented, their conscience controls them in that they can even report themselves to authorities when they break the law of mess up. They are very obedient.

The ***Other directed,*** who have misty feelings about right and wrong, when they deviate from a norm, they don't feel the guilt but if caught they feel shame. The believe it is okay to do both right and wrong as long as they are not caught in wrong.

David's effort was at some extent valid though with limitations that would require additional details but in this I found some reality because there are people in this world who believe in doing things the same way year after year with no intention to change or adopt news ways, these are the traditional oriented. We also have people living in this world who are so obedient, honest and controlled by their conscience, there life is so much affected by their intentional mistakes sometimes the conscience cannot hold the guilt they feel inside and this leads them to confession.

We also have people in this world who don't care at all, they know what is right and wrong but none matters to them. They can decide to do wrong things for some reasons and get away with it but in instances where they are caught, it causes them a huge embarrassment.

At this point I suppose you are able to identify which category of personalities you belong to as per David Riesman's suggestion.

I would like to make it clear to you that as you are reading this book there will be instances where I will be requesting you to check yourself as per a particular aspect and judge yourself, however what is most important of all is that you will have to be 100% true and honest to yourself. This is the only way you will fully benefit from this book to awaken your potential.

For everything that happens or will happen in your life begins with you. You are your own destination that is why it is a wrong idea to opt for that dangerous option of shifting blame to other parties when you fail. You must teach yourself to take full responsibility of your failures and weaknesses then take appropriate measure to make yourself better. If you can't be honest to yourself there is no way you can be honest to others. If you don't love yourself, you can't love someone else and if you claim to do it, that is hypocrisy of the highest level and a good road to self-destruction because you can never be what are not always at one point you will be forced into revealing your true self whether you like it or not but prayer should be that this happens early enough when you have an opportunity to change otherwise it is self-destruction.

*"Understanding who you are individually
is the first step to a successful potential unlock and
Judging yourself genuinely or truthfully or honestly
gives you a key to great personality development."*

Arthur Mubezi

Scenario: Here is a scenario where identical twins were brought up in the same environment and exposed to similar conditions at home. They grew up together sharing everything and loved each other madly. Later it was noticed that the two boys had very different personalities in fact on average nobody ever described the twins with similar personality traits much as their faces resembled each other. On the other hand, you could find many different people describing a particular twin with some common characteristics. So now, out of the factors we have discussed earlier what do you think could have caused that difference in personality?

The scenario of the twins suggests that even when other factors are left constant, we cannot have same personality which means that, there will always be something to uniquely differentiate us from others. The environment provides a neutral ground for other factors like the hereditary genes and character to play but the way we individually perceive and respond to the physical, social emotional, cultural among other factors that exist in our environment is what shapes personality in that case. This also explains why we can't have exactly the same personality with another person but we can share some characteristics.

The twins shared genes and environment but character defied the order because each perceived and responded differently in a similar situation and this gradually shaped their different personality based other players like emotions, thinking and mind set.

Now that we have learnt about the different factors that shape someone's personality, I want us to take another step and look at the basic principles or aspects in life that promote good personality and above all help you to awaken yourself for success by revamping your potential resting in you to gear you to success in life.
You might have heard people saying that it is impossible to change a person's nature but I can tell you that it is actually possible to change a person's nature through outstanding efforts that impact on the person's thinking, cognition, habits and character. It may not be ideal to start blaming anyone for the kind of personality you may possess, I call this shifting blame (this will be discussed in later chapters) the only good news here is that it is

possible to change your personality all you need is to adopt some of the general principles of life and allow them to take effect in your life.

Here are some of the tips that can help you to gradually develop and maintain a good personality.

Be yourself: Being something that you are not is one of the most tiresome things in life. You cannot mold yourself to fit in or be accepted in a certain class of people forever, this usually backfires since we are all unique in several ways and mind you expressing that uniqueness is what makes us interesting, so don't try to be a carbon copy of someone else because one time you will fall flat and expose your lack of legitimacy to that character you force onto yourself. Being yourself helps to identify your real weaknesses and to get help from other people around you since they will understand the true you and your weaknesses.

Always be positive: As a way of building good personality you must keep a positive mind all the time because all sensible people fancy keeping around positive minded people not the negative minded people whose work is to complain all the time and gossip without any positives. Avoid people with negative minds and keep around positive thinking people. Meanwhile you should always Keep a positive mind because a positive mind attracts more people of the kind and the more you stay with positive minded people the more you learn from them and the better you develop your personality.

Knowledge search: You need to try and develop new interest like reading books. Reading books is a very good habit as it helps to acquire more knowledge and exposure to new things such that each time you meet people you have something new to share with them. Reading books also makes you a good conversationalist and remember that good conversationalist can fit anywhere which helps you to learn of other people's opinions and ideas which add to your knowledge and eventually boost your personality as time goes by.

Meet new people: In later chapters we shall discuss about the kind of people we need to keep around us in detail but right now what you need to understand is that meeting new people whom you share a positive attitude is important because it exposes you to new ways of doing things and new cultures too, this in one way or another broadens your horizons and this automatically begins to influence your personality development through the "mirror neuron" effect.

Be the best listener: Making yourself the best listener requires you to develop the highest listening skills. It so much appealing to have someone listening to you attentively and making you feel like you are the only person in the world. If you are a good listener, you learn a lot from your surroundings. While listening to others intently you make them feel important and in turn, they do the same to you sometimes it makes them to feel so free with you and end up sharing lots of information with you. Naturally talking while someone is listening to you intently makes you feel more important and it adds to your confidence.

Get to know your personality and work on keeping it up beat because is the basis of what you may have to achieve or desire in life.

CHAPTER TWO
DISCIPLINE

Many times, we have heard and used discipline as a word which to the majority is associated with good manners. Most of the people if asked they will say to you that discipline means good manners amongst people which means that if you behave well in people then you are a disciplined person, this is partly correct but discipline is more than just social manners it goes deeper onto self-control.

I personally look at discipline as that control you gain when you enforce obedience to do whatever you are expected to do and following a particular order to do things.

Having discipline assures you of self-control that is why it is very vital to every human being. It is discipline that creates order otherwise the world will be filled with chaos all the time due to lack of discipline. Try to imagine a situation where soldiers in the army have no discipline and that anyone is free to do as they wish with their weapons.

What sort of life would it be? It is in such instances that you can see and realize how crucial it is to have discipline. The secrete about discipline that most people don't realize is the fact that discipline trains you and makes you more willing to obey or able to control different aspects of life which helps to live a smooth and happy life.

All highly successful people in the world exhibit high levels of discipline on a daily basis in order to be able to achieve their top goals, to narrow down the scope of this discussion I would like to focus a little more on self-discipline.

Self-discipline is an aggregate of **internal** and **external discipline**.
Internal discipline refers to your willpower and ability to differentiate between right and wrong.
External discipline refers to the kind of discipline that accords to social norms like following rules and laws. This is what most people are familiar with and it is what in most cases people base on to judge other people's discipline.

For anyone to become great and inspiring to people you must unremittingly show self-discipline which in turn guides you to make right decisions. Remember every decision in life is very essential because it can either make you or break you therefore, we must always toil to make rightful decisions regardless of anything. Lack of self-discipline can actually lead you into making wrong decisions simply because many times you'll end up compromising on crucial decisions which eventually destroys you completely.

Self – discipline Should be kept at the entrance of our hearts and mind because it is what makes us smart, unique and progressive in life. It is very paramount to everyone especially those who intend to achieve in life like the talented ones.

I highly doubt if there is anyone person whom God never gifted with a special talent. I am 100% sure that every human being was blessed with a special talent or skill but the reason why most people just bury and waste their talents is because, every talent requires a high level of self-discipline if you are to get the best out of it.

I will now share with you a story about my friend called Juma a soccer genius by then, he was really a talented soccer player. We played together at high school in both junior and senior teams respectively but he was exceptional in his position and unpredictable at the pitch. In fact, at this level even the coaches had less work to do with him. His creativity always made me a star in scoring goals. As we progressed from high school to other levels, we started to work with more professional coaches who had different ways of doing things as a team. I and Juma got a chance to sign for a team in the top division football league and this time it was professional football we had to sign a contract. Honestly when we were served with the contract non us read through the contract terms keenly but thank God there wasn't any problem with it. The amount that had been printed in the contract as our pay was

19

enough to cover any issues in the contract. The
excitement couldn't allow us to read beyond the figures.

The first game we played was against a very experienced
side in the top league with mature, strong and experienced
players. The game was so hard for us actually we barely
featured in the game at the pitch and for the first time we
were substituted from the pitch for poor performance I
suppose in a competitive game. We really tried our best
but the biggest challenge was that we were so weak our
fitness was rated at 20% by the coach after the game.
We lost the game 0:2 at our home ground. The coach
called us aside and said to us that we are good players
but we needed to work on our fitness to become better. In
the next training session, we had to run around the pitch
for two hours constantly before kicking on the ball. This
was honestly a very hard task for us and to worsen the
situation the coach said that it was going to be our routine
at every training session. We were surely disappointed
and felt like the man was just against us. The next training
session was a day before another game. The coach called
us and said that our fitness was now worth 10mins on

pitch so he said he would field us for only 10 minutes in that game. It was disappointing actually Juma just walked off angry and demoralized but I personally respected the coach so much because he had won many titles as a coach in other clubs so I believed in him though I felt I was fit enough for at least a full half. When the time came during the game I was so much on tension because I wanted to prove a point to the coach in those few minutes I'll get. Finally, I got on pitch with ten minutes left and with God's grace I was able to score an equalizing goal for my team in the last minutes. Honestly the few minutes I played were so magical and made the funs to think that if I had entered earlier, I would have scored more goals, my friend Juma was given about 5 minutes on pitch for which his morale was so down because he was used to starting in the line-up. The coach maintained his decision that we had to work harder and now we had to run for 2hr and 30mins constantly and play for 30mins only during the training sessions. The next training session Juma didn't turn up claiming he wasn't feeling well but I knew he was fine. He missed the training for three days then showed up on the fourth day which was a day to another game, When

Juma came he was stopped from training with the squad but the coach asked him to run around at his pace. Juma told the coach that he was not ready to run as though he is preparing for a marathon, he tried to force himself on pitch but the coach insisted and finally suspended Juma. This was the first time something like this happened to us, at earlier levels the coaches never used to mind us and we could train for as long as we wanted but at this point it was mandatory and hard. After Juma's suspension of two weeks, he returned and the coach told him that he hard to work on his fitness for a full week without training with squad. Juma was not happy with this and he had no patience left so he opted for a release to leave the club. I tried to talk to him to change his mind but he had made up his mind to leave, I never met Juma soon again for some time, he joined a club where he was promised to play first team football but the club was so disorganized and eventually it was disqualified from the league in which we could get a chance to meet and play against each other. I met Juma after three years and he told me he had stopped playing soccer because he had no time and love for running all the time and training everyday as a must and also controlling his free style of play. His statement really touched me so much knowing how much potential he had in him when it came to soccer especially dribbling and passing the ball, he was superb. Within that time at my club I was able to adapt to the system and also I became a better player with full qualities, we won championships and played in international and regional tournaments, where I got injured with an arm string that finally saw me off the game till now otherwise it was a very good experience to play at a professional level. Juma despite of his wonderful talent, he never won any major trophies at a professional level yet I am sure he should have played at the national team if he had just exhibited some self-discipline or control like I did. I learnt self-discipline from my mother though by then I never knew that it is self-discipline but she always urged us to be best listeners and be patient always with new situations, this is what kept me going and actually I made it. To cut the story short the main point for sharing this story is to show you how much damage that lacking self-control can cause us. When you lack self-control, you are bound to make wrong decisions which can affect your life forever.

"Talent without discipline is like
an octopus on roller skates"

There is plenty of movements but you never know if it is
going forward, backward or sideways.

Self- discipline is very critical in your life because it allows
you to feel your individuality, your inner strength, your
talent and also a feeling that you are a master not a slave
of your own thoughts and emotions. I strongly believe that
Juma's weakness was lack of self- discipline which would
have given him patience, respect and a clear decision-
making pattern that would not bury his special talent.
People who lack self-control don't always mind about long
term effects of their actions and this was the case with
Juma, I don't think he would just leave that opportunity we
had got to work with one of the best coaches in the
country. This explains why it is very critical to have self-
discipline especially if you need to achieve a goal. Also, If
Juma had self-discipline he would be able to understand
that every coach has his way of building a team and
whatever he does he does it for good of his players. I was
able to understand the importance of the body fitness in

sports and at some point, I started pushing myself into fitness training to become stronger and better.

"Discipline is a bridge between goals and accomplishments."

Mubezi Arthur D

This means that once you have your goals set, all you need is discipline to help you accomplish them.

Self-control or self-discipline is a very fundamental skill to have as a human being because it is not good enough to possess good qualities as a person, what is most important is having the ability to control and or manage those qualities.

Self –control is not only about depriving or restricting yourself but it is actually about managing conflict and making decisions that match your personal goals.

Look back through all the actions and decisions you have taken in your life then closely analyze how they have impacted on your life. You can simply sight out the big mistakes you ever made in the past and examine why you decided to take the kind of action or decision which turned out to be bad. I am sure you will definitely realize that there was another better option that you didn't take up. That is what we call poor decision making where you have a better option but you end up taking on the wrong one. The most common cause for wrong decisions is lack of self-discipline because if you don't have self-discipline you easily compromise in your decisions at the expense of the right decision. Therefore, I would like to encourage you to develop and strengthen your self-discipline such that you become a better decision maker and a better person. You might be wondering how you can build and strengthen your self – discipline but here are some tips that you can adopt;

Make promises and ensure that you fulfill them. A promise is a commitment therefore failure to fulfill means lack of commitment and that is lack of discipline.

Align your actions and behavior with your thoughts. This means that you have to make **genuine** efforts to ensure that all your right thoughts are matched with right actions and behavior regardless of anything.

Avoid or resist any negative behavior. You should always ensure that you only focus on the positive attributes in your life and soberly avoid the urge that pushes you into adopting a negative behavior that will cost you a lot.

Keep your body and mind in shape. You can easily achieve this through doing physical exercise. We believe that a healthy mind lives in a healthy body so by doing this you will be able to keep your body and mind upbeat.

There are several reasons why we should mind our discipline. I know most of the people have heard about this concept of discipline but I suppose a few of them understand it well that is why they attach it to social conduct only yet discipline in actual sense goes beyond that. I have followed various speeches and counseling sessions on discipline cases but they are all full of "don'ts" rather than "dos". I find this so weird; I think it's also the reason why such sessions are not so effective, I would personally rather tell people what they ought to do to exhibit good discipline than what not to do to exhibit discipline. It is better to learn what you have to do than learning what you don't have to do. I'll give an example during the COVID-19 pandemic in 2020 if you communicated to people only the don'ts you would leave many questions an answered for example you would say don't cough or sneeze amidst people, don't touch you're your eyes, nose and mouth, avoid crowds etc. The questions would arise what if I can't hold it back or how can I clean my nose, eyes and mouth without touching them? And if I avoid crowds am I safe with 2, 3 people? But look at this if the Dos are communicated. Here you would say You must cover your mouth and nose while coughing or sneezing to block the virus from spreading, you must use clean tissue to clean your nose and eyes, wash your hands all the time with soap etc. keep distancing yourself from people. I think you can notice the difference between negative and positive communications.

 My point in this is that we ought to be positive when communicating certain crucial information to avoid leaving behind an answered question that may trouble the targeted audience. Usually as people communicate about discipline, they concentrate more on the things we do that exhibit indiscipline rather than the things we must do that exhibit discipline. In school teachers will tell children fighting and abusing is a bad habit, which is good to know but if I don't fight and or abuse what do I do in such a situation that calls for anger? That is the question that is always left behind. A positive caution would be something like; We must always solve our differences amicably this will not leave a question but a challenge to find out the amicable ways of solving issues which is positive.

I would like to share some of the importance or the benefits of having discipline.

Discipline helps you achieve your goals it removes all the would-be destruction in your life since it gives you the ability to choose between right and wrong.

Discipline gives you the strength to resist temptations which may affect your life.

Discipline makes you a master and not a slave of your own thoughts. This means that it gives you control over your thoughts and emotions as well hence giving you more confidence.

Discipline trains your mind and character to have self-control and practice obedience which helps you to make good decision.

Discipline makes the society enjoyable as it promotes good human behavior. Imagine if there is no discipline in the army completely allowing them to use their guns and bombs in any way they want. That is the power of discipline.

When you identify the kind of life that you want to live or once you identify the specific goal you want to achieve in life, you have to ensure that you adopt the actual discipline it requires. You may have to adjust both your internal and external discipline to match.

There was a time when Inzikuru and Kiprotich didn't matter in our lives at all then also came a time when the two mattered to everyone in the country and the world as well. That is what happens when you awaken yourself for success. Awakening yourself means unlocking your potential to bring out the best in you so as to achieve a particular goal.

Not until you bring out the best in you that you will matter in life otherwise you will pass through the world without living even a micro legacy to your name. We are all filled with potential and special talent to inspire and appeal to the world but sometimes our personality blocks us especially when we dock in negative thinking, fixed mindset, poor attitude and laziness. No one in this world has ever succeeded with such characteristics active in their personality. If you have failed somewhere or you know of someone who has failed somewhere closely watch them and see if those characters will miss in their personality.

If you find yourself in the same boat of such people don't morn because you are yet to be transformed through this book. Inzikuru and Kiprotich who won gold medals in crucial international engagements never woke up from sleep and went ahead to win the championships, No. they had to go through a chain of things as they prepared for the races. None of us even knows what they went through during preparation but we all know that they won gold medals for our country. That is why I say that when you identify a specific goal that you want to achieve, take full responsibility over it and count any failures to yourself. This is where self-discipline comes in, if you don't have it you will only end at identifying the goal and lack the courage to copy up with the necessary discipline hence you will start compromising with your laziness, poor attitude and negative thinking. Inzikuru and Kiprotich must have exhibited high levels of self-discipline to encourage themselves train hard every day, forego some social relationships, money etc. they had to sacrifice a lot so as to concentrate on achieving their goal and dream in athletics. It was self-discipline they exhibited that helped them to control the would be inner and outer disruptions through taking right decisions, actions keeping the right attitude and perseverance. A point to carry home here is that without discipline success becomes a myth in your life. Discipline does not only entail social behavior amidst people but it goes deep into aspects like ability to resist temptations and disruptions that may cause you to channel away from your main goal.

"To be a champion of your own life
you must possess maximum discipline
in all aspects of life."
Mubezi Arthur Denis

CHAPTER THREE
SELF EXAMINATION

It is a very good practice to keep on self-examining yourself about the different things you encounter in life. In life we encounter and go through so many things which provoke our response and reaction in order to overcome them. It is some of those challenges that eventually shape our personality and also determine our level of success. We have talked about the environment as a very critical factor in shaping personality yet it has various components that we need to understand and examine ourselves on how those components are impacting on us.

Self-examination is basically based on your personal observation, reaction and responses in life at a given point in time. There are some questions that need to be answered at every point in time because they provide you with a clear vision of your endeavors.

This question "Who are you? "seems obvious to many people but it is a very crucial parameter in life to know who you are especially if you intend to achieve at a particular level. Knowing and understanding who you are, is a very important aspect in life because it helps you to determine your strength, weaknesses, interests, ambitions etc. which eventually trigger your desire to achieve specific goals. Answering this "Who you are?" question goes beyond just knowing your name, age, gender etc. and it digs deeper into your personality therefore if you don't know your personality then you are like a balloon in the air where it has no control over itself so it lets its weight and wind to decide for it where to go and land regardless. In real life this is a point where you have no purpose for life, or when you are hopeless and so you have lost grip of your life. It is a point where you have left the situation and the surrounding to decide your destination.

The reason why you need to self-examine yourself is because it helps you to know and understand yourself better in terms of strength, weaknesses, interests, etc. Self-examination requires you to be totally genuine and honest to yourself otherwise if you compromise with yourself at this point, you will be pinning yourself on a cross. The major aspects to consider in self-examination include; character, strength and weaknesses which can give you a better explanation as to why you have failed or succeeded in some areas something that actually clears your vision and directs you to becoming better and achieve more.

Once you manage to identify your strong points which are your strength, you'll get an idea of what you are capable of doing. Knowing your strength will also help you identify how much you have utilized your strength, go ahead and look at what you have achieved in life so far by putting your strength to play. In case you have achieved something, that is good but the question is, "Is it the best you can get out of yourself? Or is it all you need to achieve in life?" On the other hand, if you realize that you have never achieved anything in life much as you have that strength you have identified, it means that you haven't got yourself any seriousness so you need to wake up yourself and get going, leave the comfort zone and unlock your potential.

Whichever situation it is above, you should not find contentment in the little you have got which does not actually match your strengths, skills and potential.

My caution is that once you manage to identify your strengths and capability, do not tailor your goals to match your strengths because that will not push you to high level. All you need is to set yourself bigger and challenging tasks that can move you from one level to another.

Many people sympathize with themselves and set simple goals that they can achieve with no serious effort involved, such people consider themselves achievers of highfliers yet they never actually progress to higher levels. Any successful person should always aim higher and work for the best all through. If you have been the kind who settles for less and gets contentment in small attainments it is time to revise your rules of engagement in the battle for total success. Push yourself out and achieve bigger goals that match your full potential without sympathizing with yourself. Let the sky be your limit otherwise your potential is or can only be limited by you.

God blessed everyman with a special talent or skill to give him a competitive advantage over others. Everyone is born with a special talent or skill that is meant to make you better than others as well as giving you the potential to achieve something special in life therefore if you have never achieved any major goal yet from your self-examination you managed to raise strong points as your strength just know there is a problem that you need to sort out immediately.

The unprecedented success of our age mates or people known to us is not meant to demoralize or define us as failures in life but it is supposed to encourage us, give us hope and also act as our reference to prove that success is a journey that anyone can travel. Look around and see what other people in the same age bracket as you have achieved a head of you and task yourself to find out why it is like that especially after you have identified your actual strengths, weaknesses and own personality.

As mentioned earlier that truthfulness and honesty are very crucial when conducting self-examination, be sure that if you compromise with yourself when doing this then you are chasing after wind. A false representation of yourself will lead you to hell so please practice self-discipline and be genuine as you list your strengths, weaknesses, special skill or talent. Being honest to yourself helps you to identify your actual weaknesses and where you go wrong then probably start from there. Sometimes we make mistakes and we fail to acknowledge them which sometimes turns out to be a serious problem in our lives therefore during self-examination if you happen to realize instances where you made mistakes, it is very vital that you acknowledge those mistakes then pick out a positive lesson from such mistakes. Again, if you are the kind who finds option in shifting blame for their failures to other parties you are doomed but for now avoid lamenting and unproductive regrets, just keep a positive attitude. As a matter of fact, experience is the best teacher and through mistakes we learn so the best thing to do is to acknowledge our mistakes, learn from them and become better people. The mistakes we make become learning points when we acknowledge them.

Here is a question, how easy is it for you to acknowledge your mistakes or to take blames in good faith? Many times, people look for excuses to protect themselves from taking blame for failing or the mistakes they make yet it is more beneficial when we learn to acknowledge our mistakes and take the blame in good faith.

> *"Acknowledging your own mistakes*
> *and accepting to learn from them*
> *makes you a hero of your own life."*

Mubezi Arthur

Look back in your life and pick up one incident which you think it happened because you made a mistake or took a wrong decision then go ahead and review the negative effects it caused in your life, then basing on those negative effects come up with a strong positive point to pick out as a lesson.

There are various things that we can learn from the different people around us therefore as you conduct self-examination ask yourself what lessons you have learnt from other people's mistakes and success stories remember human beings are components of the environment so we need to consider their impact on us and this is one of the ways.

In our daily life we encounter a number of challenges especially as we grow right from childhood, however we all encounter different challenges and in instances where people face similar challenges many times their responses differ simply because life has no uniform formula for solving problems or facing challenges. Therefore, you need to look at what other people are going through with a keen interest of learning how different people respond to different situations. This will help you to understand better how our own responses, reactions and perceptions can either make us or break us as you see other people's progress after taking certain critical decision in their lives. Sometimes as you are meditating upon your life you may pick out one or two scenarios from other people's lives relevant to you and ask yourself how best you would respond to it.

The other aspect to consider during self-examination is your skills, talent and interest. We agree that everyone has a special skill, a talent or special interest where they

can perform best. It is very important for you to identify
which special skill, talent or interest you possess simply
because this helps to identify your area of interest and
once you have discovered your area of operation then you
will be in position to set clear and specific goals to achieve
and this will further help you to determine the kind of
discipline you need to adopt and exhibit in order to
achieve such a goal.

Certainly, after Inzikuru and Kiprotich identified their
talents they developed belief in themselves that they can
run better than anyone else so they set their bars high to
become world champions and that is what they had in
mind as they trained their bodies to be fit for that
challenge. I am very sure they had to do a lot to put
themselves in shape and they had to bear with all that so
as to achieve their goal. They had to exhibit a high level of
self- discipline which in turn helped them to remain
focused on their primary goal rather than losing focus to
disruptions and other challenges. Therefore, once you
have discovered your special talent or skill please give it
priority and exercise self-discipline so as to achieve the
goal you will set. Examine yourself and see what qualities

are missing in you that are crucial for your success. Take a step to understand the rules of the game for example find out if you have the kind of discipline it requires, if you don't have it, are you are able to adjust or adopt to it? if it requires a particular skill do you have it and if not are you able to learn it? Answering those questions require maximum honesty to yourself because you know yourself more than anyone else otherwise any compromise will lead you to self-destruction.

Your power is triggered through genuine self-examination which helps to identify your actual strength, weakness, talent or special skills and once you have identified those aspects, you will now know your actual potential and you will be able to set a clear and specific goal.

"Knowing what you can do best
through talent, special skills and or special interest
opens your mind to golden opportunities."

Mubezi Arthur

In a nut shell I would like to emphasize that when you are doing self-examination be 100% honest and true to yourself, do not compromise on any aspect or else you will be sailing to a self-destruction mission.

"You can only help yourself
by being true and honest to yourself."

Mubezi Arthur

CHAPTER FOUR
MINDSET AND ATTITUDE

Mindset is basically a class of things or characteristics someone develops to live a particular life style. The mindset plays a very big role in setting and building our attitude. In this chapter we shall talk about the main forms of mindset briefly such that you can understand how a wrong mindset can affect your success and personality. There are two main forms of mindset; *Fixed mindset* and *Growth mindset also called the positive mindset.*

Fixed Mindset

A fixed mindset is one that is not willing or ready to change even when situations change. The other way to express this is saying that this kind of mindset is static. People with such kind of mindset believe that their abilities and understanding are relatively fixed, so _you are either good at something_ or _you are not_ and you cannot change your qualities which means that to them any additional effort to change or learn something new is a waste of time.

A fixed mind is like a ball placed in a bowel no matter which side you roll it to it will always roll back to the bottom and settle. The people with this kind of mindset find comfort in a specific state of mind where they feel that everything in life is in equilibrium; there is no need to change anything in fact they feel more secure leaving things unchanged from the way they have always been done because they are scared of what may come out of new ways.

I would say that fixed minded people think and believe that what is not known to them does not exist or if it does then it is not relevant in their life.
Some of the characteristics of fixed minded people include;

Fear and or hatred of challenges. Fixed minded people hate and avoid challenges all the time thinking that challenges will push them out of their comfort zone so it is better to avoid the challenges and remain in their usual state of "equilibrium".

Fixed minded people are feeble, they are not persistent they give up so easily. Sometimes when they choose to try something new, they do it while "praying" for a challenge to arise and the moment a challenge comes up that is the end no more attempt because any additional effort will be a waste of time and energy according to them.

Hate and ignore criticism. The other thing to note about fixed minded people is that they so much hate and ignore criticism. They will always want to look smart even where they know nothing just because they hate looking "foolish". They are always right, what they know is what everyone should embrace and whatever they don't know is not worth knowing or it should be perceived their way.

Contentment in very small things. Fixed minded people get contentment in very small things and in most cases, they fail to achieve their actual goals. That is why you can hardly achieve big goals when you possess such a mindset.

Lastly but not least, fixed minded people are so envious and jealousy. This really beats my understanding because if they are scared of challenges through which most people achieve their targets and goals why then should they envy those who successfully meet their targets? Probably they think that everyone must think the same way they do and achieve the same as they do but this can never happen. There is also this poor thinking in them that "talent alone is enough to help you achieve, no need for additional effort" so they sleeve their talents and never take a step to develop them. This is stupid!

Looking back to David Riesman's theory I think these fixed minded people are good examples of the traditional oriented category who believe in doing things the way they have always been done even when such ways have not been successful in some cases.

Growth mindset

This is the kind of mindset that is very much ready and willing to change so as to fit a given situation. People with this kind of mindset which I believe is the right mindset are always progressive in whatever they do.
This kind of mindset drives your desire to learn from life as

life itself is not static, it has various dynamics from which we have to learn and adopt to, where necessary so as to fit in some situations. That is why people with a growth mindset which is ready and willing to change are never left behind by any trends.

People with this kind of mindset usually acknowledge and realize that challenges are part of life and with that, they are eager and willing to face them rather than avoiding them like the fixed minded people. Some of the common characteristics of the growth mindset or the open mindset include but not limited to;

Embracing challenges. The people with a growth mindset embrace and realize that challenges are part of life so they face them with a positive attitude.

Determination. The people with a growth mindset are determined to fight any setbacks. They don't allow any setback to disrupt their endeavors unlike the fixed minded people who let one setback in their life to define them forever.

Willingness to learn. People with a growth mindset *willingly learn from other people* who are better that them in some field and they go ahead to ask how certain things are done especially when they admire such a thing.

Hangout with positive thinking people. People with a growth mindset always *look out or hangout with positive thinking people or the wise ones.* They so much avoid people with negative minds and attitude because they have nothing to learn from them.

Persistence. People with a growth mindset are very persistent. They possess the diehard spirit of not just giving up in life that is why in most cases they are progressive.

That is briefly what we can say about mindset but as you examine yourself on which kind of mindset you possess, remember the number one principle of being honest and truthful to yourself because it is the only way you can benefit from this book. If you have been possessing a fixed mind where you have been comfortably avoiding challenges, avoiding to adopt to new ways of doing things, surrounding yourself with people who never add value to you and feeling lazy to start something, it is time to change and develop a brand new mindset. Meanwhile if you have been having a growth mindset am sure you have realized how much potential you have that you have probably not been putting to use. Reflect the true growth mindset you have and be sure of success and or better life.

ATTITUDE
While opening this chapter we mentioned that Mindset plays a very big role in setting and building our attitude. Attitude is also a very crucial determinant of someone's success and progress in life. Your attitude plays a very big role to enable your success, if you ever possess a negative or poor attitude towards anything positive, you are doomed to register any success in that line. This means that if you truly wish to succeed in life, your number one task is to develop a positive attitude and this is how it works; When you have a strong attitude of optimism, expectancy and enthusiasm, your opportunities will grow and the problems will definitely shrink.

Those who are in leadership, attitude draws more people to your side and it also encourages them to do their best whenever called up on a particular task.

"A poor or Negative attitude
is a direct route to failure
but a mere positive attitude
is a secret key to successful ways."

Mubezi Arthur

The good news about our own attitude is that we can control it and engineer it where it is due through adopting some measures that can keep it upbeat. Having the right attitude makes us better people, better leaders, better achievers and good examples to others through our success. The question is, how can you change your attitude or build a positive attitude in your life? Earlier I stressed that the number one task for anyone who wants to succeed and achieve their goals in life is to build and maintain a positive attitude. Some of the ways through which you can create and maintain a desired positive attitude include but not limited to;

Having an open mindset. The open mindset allows to learn and take up new ways of doing things where necessary. Such ways may make work easier or give you an opportunity to learn something new that will make you better hence boosting your attitude. Doing things, the same old ways is very depressing at times even when such ways have been successful at times, they become so boring and obvious which depresses you and eventually affects your attitude negatively. Therefore, an open mind will boost your attitude yet the fixed mind will lock you down to doing things the same old ways something that will depress you and demoralize you in some cases thus affecting your attitude. Someone once compared success to athletics saying that "if you don't stretch yourself every day you gradually become slow and brittle." Meaning that it is a good practice to keep on trying new things and taking on new challenges rather than assuming that you have it all.

Have purposeful actions and movements. You should always have purposeful actions if you want to build and maintain a positive attitude. Part of this will be mentioned as we talk about reaction and actions. It is very important that we mind much about how we respond and react to situations; in this I mean that do your best to persistently take on positive reactions because they result into positive and strong actions that can save your major goals. The more you achieve your targets, the more you develop and strengthen your attitude. Whenever you realize that the action you are to take has no connection to your main goal or maybe the connection is weak, scrap it off from your to-do list because aimless activities and movements just waste your time and energy. Such disappointments from those aimless activities and movements affect your attitude on a negative note. So always ensure that you have a purpose for every action and movement if you need to create and maintain a strong positive attitude.

Don't expect results for the actions you take. This aspect is quite logical you must read it carefully to understand it better. I know you can't imagine taking action yet you don't expect results but this is how it absolutely works; Definitely we must always take on the rightful and purposeful actions good enough to give us good results but at the back of your mind convince yourself to believe that the action taken is one way and you don't guarantee yourself with the expected results. Naturally as we take decisions we look at the results we want to achieve however when you set all your eyes on the result and they don't come out as you expected, many times you are disappointed and in some cases your attitude towards such a thing falls completely that is why I emphasize that take your best shot, know why you are taking that action but don't fixate to the results. In other words, be expectant of both positive and negative results but let non distort the "equilibrium" of your state of mind. By so doing, you will be able to maintain a positive attitude. Your expectation for results should always be equal for both the expected and unexpected results if your attitude is to be kept positive.

One time I had an encounter with a very good friend of mine whom I met at church. She was a spiritual hero and perfect in that line, that is how I actually looked at her in that manner. However, as time went on, I realized that she concentrated more on her spiritual life and ignored her physical personality as she prayed to God for wisdom and knowledge. She probably forgot to pray about the gift of self-discipline in her physical life. Much as the biblical teachings are very clear and strict on the elements of; forgiving and forgetting, treating your neighbor as you would wish to be treated as well as loving your neighbor as you love yourself, I am certain that she did not receive the grace to put that into play. On the side of physical personality, she lacked self-discipline, she had poor attitude and she was a slave to her own emotions and thoughts. At one time she had a misunderstanding with her boyfriend claiming that he had accused her for being lose and going out with several guys which was a very simple case because the guy could have felt un easy as he saw the girlfriend constantly posting other guys pictures on one of her social media profiles. After listening to her carefully I told that the guy's reaction was natural and that he had a point to worry but this to her sounded like I was on supporting the guy. The worst came when I advised her to face the her guy directly and tell him that his accusation had hurt her so much so they could talk things out but her response and reaction showed me who truly she was character wise and mind set. Actually, her response and reaction revealed her true personality to me. She told me that *she can't waste her time talking to the guy because he hurt her so much with his accusation and even though* she *doesn't care what other people say, she does what makes her happy not what people expect her to do and* **she is tired of doing good yet others don't do her good**. Based on that I realized that she lacks all the basics of life we have so far discussed to this point for example She doesn't know who she is, her personality, she has a fixed mind, she lacks self-discipline and has a very poor attitude. She has accepted to be a slave of her own thoughts. Try to relate her statement with my prior description of her spiritual mark and see if she possesses any of the major principles of Christianity yet she looks a first-class material in spiritual life. I am quite certain that if you have been following our discussions from the start you can out rightly judge her attitude. When I asked her to critically think about what she was doing, she got so angry thinking that I am supporting her enemy so I left her because I knew how she behaves when she is angry. Many times, what people speak out when they are angry reflects their actual personality that is why self-control is crucial in our lives.

The point I wanted to bring out from this story is how not knowing who you are and lacking self-control can affect your life and also to confirm to you how dangerous it is to fixate actions on results especially where she says that *she is tired of doing good to people yet they don't do good for her.* I asked her if she really does good where she expected to get back good but she couldn't answer. This is a very good example of how putting all your eyes on results when you take action can disappoint you. Doing good is a very good action but expecting good from whoever you do it to, is heart breaking and will affect your attitude seriously.

I also realized that it is important to engage in purposeful discussions because they can help you identify which kind of people you associate with and how to deal with each and this can help you to reduce on disappointments from such people which may affect your attitude negatively.

Setbacks review. Another way through which you can build and maintain a positive attitude is reviewing your setbacks with an aim of improving your skills or building and maintaining a positive attitude. Many times, when people are rejected or when they fail, they feel so bad and their attitudes in the same way is affected but the truth is that, that rejection and or failure is a golden opportunity for you to improve on your performance or being. Therefore, in such a situation all you need to do is to sit back and see what or where went wrong then identify what you need to do to improve, bearing in mind that the results you want to achieve are reflected in what you receive. Reviewing setbacks helps you improve and maintain a positive attitude.

> _"The results you want to see_
> _are reflected in what you receive_
> _don't fixate on a particular result."_

Meet new people. This basically means associating with people from different walks of life who actually share your positive attitude. Science shows that our brains automatically imitate the behavior of the people around us because of something called *mirror neuron* therefore you should always surround yourself with positive thinkers and avoid those who are excessively negative. Positive people will encourage you, challenge you, introduce you to new ways of doing things etc. in so doing you will build or maintain a positive attitude.

Frequently say thank you. Saying thank you to people more frequently for their gifts to you regardless of the size may seem so obvious even when it is as trivial as a grin but it is a very powerful tool to build your attitude of appreciation. The attitude of gratitude is achieved through more than just knowing what is exceptional in your life but also how you receive offers from other people's lives as they express their appreciation. You must be aware of how it feels when someone appreciates you, so when you thank people you will also be thanked and it will further contribute to a good interpersonal relationship with people you appreciate which will cause them to love, care and encourage you when the spirit goes down hence helping you build or maintain a strong positive attitude.

Acknowledge that people differ

In the same way you must also embrace the fact that human beings differ a lot and therefore it makes no sense for you to become miserable simply because someone else has failed to do something the way you would exactly do it or because someone has a different vision from what you have. These two small things have the power that can influence your attitude if you don't make them part of you.

CHAPTER FIVE
LESSONS IN LIFE

Life is a school in itself and it uses its challenges to test us at different levels right from childhood, that is why we say that in life "Experience is the best teacher". There are special challenges you face at each level of your life and the moment you overcome such challenges you automatically advance to the next level therefore it is prudent to pick up a lesson from every challenges you encounter in life.

The uniqueness about life as a school is that it has no formal curriculum to follow but it presents different challenges to different people based on their personality, character and situation. Many times, I have heard people saying that life is not fair but that is just because they look at the social differences like; different social classes commonly used in social and market research by researchers. Instances where one person struggles to get 10000shs yet another person is spending it on her nails at ago is what people call life being unfair but let me show you the other side of it and you realize that actually life is fair. I'll use the social classes which are based on income, education level, expenditure, etc.; AB class is for the rich the top most, CD class can also be called the middle class and finally DE class is for poor and the poorest respectively. I will not go into details of the classes but I just want to show you that with all that in place, life uses its fair scale to present challenges to each person based on their ability or in this case I'll say based on the class they belong to that is why you can never find a DE class person having a challenge that requires him/her billions of shillings to solve yet a top challenge for the DE class may not even be realized as a challenge by the AB class person. So generally, each person is faced by challenges of their size. This is what I mean by life being fair, it cannot throw you a challenge beyond your capability all you need to do is being positive and acknowledging that the challenge is meant to push you to another level in life and to add on your life experience since after dealing with them positively we record them as lessons in life and move on.

As you look forward to awakening your potential it is very essential and helpful to meditate up on the lessons you learn from the challenges you go through, while relating them with your personal goals. See what you have failed to do, mark out the lesson learnt and move with a positive attitude. However, it is also important to understand that we don't live in a vacuum, we live on earth where there are many other creatures that we can learn from. You can take advantage of what other people go through to try and analyze how they respond to certain challenges in their lives then derive your own positive lessons from their situations to put yourself in better position knowledge wise. Make your time productive try to sink yourself into lessons each time you look into other people's situations but do not look for a reason to make you comfortable because you seem better-off.

I mentioned earlier that challenges and failures are part of life and they are meant to push us to other levels in life therefore each time you fail, be true to yourself and acknowledge it, find out where you went wrong pick out the lesson and work on it to better yourself. You may also ask yourself why you think some people have failed in certain areas of life or previous success then task yourself to list the reasons you think that made them fail then figure out what would have been the best thing for them to do. All those lessons you learn from such experiences are very helpful especially when it comes to awakening your potential.

I suppose you have ever seen people who are supported by others to start up a business, you may be right to call them lucky but the fact that you can't determine how lucky you are the best thing to do is to look at those other factors that may have convinced the other people to support that person and also partly analyze that person's character and personality, Pick out the positives.

Just as I have mentioned above, value your time always by using it to learn more and spending time with the right people. It is very crucial to effectively spend time knowing who needs much of your time and how much time nevertheless? If you spend more time with non-progressive people and negative minded people you are into a dangerous venture in fact it is more dangerous than COVID-19 and Ebola combined. Avoid wasting time as much as you can with people who don't add any value to you otherwise you are daring a suicide mission. Remember life is a school we said; if you cannot learn from what happens around you or other people around you, you are likely to trade your life to failure.

 At this point look back in your life and sight out your biggest challenge so far, if you don't have any you may get one that was faced by someone around you which you think would be big for you and analyze how you managed it or failed to handle it then ask yourself whether it was your response that triggered the action or vice versa. In other words, what is the justification for the result; is it the way you responded to the challenge that solved it or the way you acted on it?

Sometime people get confused when I mention those two terms *reaction* and *action* in relation to facing challenges but basically this is the slightest difference; *reaction* means how you immediately respond or perceive a situation then *action* means exactly what you do to solve the problem. I personally think that reaction is very crucial because it is what actually determines which action to take.

Scenario: If a snake showed up in your living room as you are watching TV what would you do first; run outside the house, sit and watch its movement or you would walk straight to catch and probably take it outside. These are all responses not actions some scientists call them reflexes on the other side beating the snake to death, or forcing it outside the room and ignoring it are actions that result from one of the reactions. Therefore, a reaction has no connection to the challenge (passive) but an action directly connects with the challenge (active). The reaction comes immediately after identifying a challenge this involves impacting on aspects of feeling, emotion, thoughts etc. before you take any step, the impact on the mentioned aspects guides you on which action to take that is why I say that reaction is very crucial. A wrong reaction is likely to drive to a wrong action and this is where the element of "Think before you act." comes in.

Always stay calm on receipt of any challenge and take time to think through all the possible options of actions before you act.

In our scenario of the snake; if you choose to run outside the house probably the snake can find a hiding for itself and this becomes more dangerous and time wasting if you are to look for it in the house. If you choose to walk straight and catch it or kill it, it will notice you as an enemy and a threat to its life so it will put on its battle combat ready for your attack and if you're not brave enough you may miss it and waste a lot of energy pulling away chairs and everything to hunt it down. Then finally if you choose to watch its movement, you could be able to see where It camps in the house if it does and deal with it at once, you will be sure that it doesn't camp in the house or if it has its habitat in the house you will be able see it and destroy all at once including young ones in case it had.

*"Keep calm when a challenge comes your way
and always think before you act."*

Mubezi Arthur

Exercise high levels of self-control once you get a challenge don't fear or avoid challenges but in steady embrace them and use them as learning sessions in life.

Find time and think about a situation where you had to take a tough action. Analyze it now once again and see whether your reaction and the action you took were the best available options to take. What were the lessons then and what are the lessons now?

CHAPTER SIX
UNDERSTANDING PEOPLE

In our earlier chapters we learnt that the environment plays a very big role in shaping our personality. We also stated that the environment has a number of components that contribute to personality development among which we mentioned *people*.

It is true, living on earth we are not living in a vacuum so we are exposed to a number of things that influence our being and personality either positively or negatively. In this chapter I will only concentrate on people around us. The people around you are so crucial in determining your success or personality; they may pull you down or support you to success. That is why it is imperative that you clearly identify which kind of people you need to keep around you. Knowing who should be around you and who you should be around helps you to eliminate and avoid people who will negatively affect your life and even waste your valuable time.

Once you have clearly identified the right people to keep around you and those you personally need to keep around them, keep monitoring their progress, character and engage in healthy talks that benefit you while you are with them. It is not a sin if you borrow some of their good traits that can make you a better person. In fact, it is a very good idea to once awhile meditate upon what you have learnt from people around you and how much they have impacted on you. If you don't see any positive impact in your life after keeping around certain people for some time just know there is a problem to check.

Of course, you must be keeping around those people who inspire you such that you are constantly provoked to work harder and be better. You must also be able to identify the different ways in which the people around you inspire you especially the ones you choose to keep around them.

Here are some of the actual reasons why we should keep people around us; to learning from them, inspiring us, encouraging and supporting us in anyway so if you realize that some people are not offering you any of the mentions above, think less and just off-load that baggage and find better people who can help you progress. I want to encourage you to also engage with people who once made it to the top and may be things fell apart for some reasons this can help you understand why they dropped off the radar and thus you will be able to understand what failed them and it will count to your lessons. In business when your immediate competitor closes down, it is not wise to celebrate the closure but it is important for you to understand why the closure. There is no need to celebrate if you don't know the actual reasons why they have closed. You need to find out why and use that information to protect yourself from such mistakes or weaknesses that could have caused them to close.

The other thing to mention here is your relationship with the people around you. The question will always be "How do you relate with the people around you?" This is a fundamental question because your relationship with people really matters a lot that is why you need to learn and know how to relate with people. It is essential that you keep relationships with people healthy and one of the ways is by treating each person with due respect in their different capabilities. Keeping healthy relationships is very important because the more you do it the more you appeal to those people and of course the more you appeal to them the more they will be willing to support you, advise you and encourage you. This is the kind of connection you need in life, having people who are willing to drive your attempt to be a better person. Avoid losing good relationships for no good reason and keep all valuable relationships healthy otherwise if you can't do that, then your plotting a homicide. You need people around you no man is an island but actually the island is also surrounded by water which qualifies it to be an island otherwise if it breaks its relationship with water and it pushes water away from around it then is seizes to be an island. This means that its existence as an Island is based on water around it. Therefore, just as the island needs water around it to be called an island, you really need people around you to support your journey to success, however not just people but progressive people.

Lastly about this point of understanding the people around you I want to emphasize that do your best to keep all helpful and progressive people around you, understand them well, respect them and as you do that also keep assessing their roles and impact in your life. This will further help you to awaken your potential meritoriously.

During my research I came across JUNG's personality types which I think can be helpful to you as you try to understand the nature of people who stay around you and how to approach them probably. Of course, it is widely accepted that we have extraverts and introverts but Jung goes ahead to break down each of those two types stating the specific characteristics for each category as summarized below;

EXTRAVERTS

Extraverted Sensation
These people are realistic; making few errors; good assimilation of details; experiencing each moment of life, enjoying the good things of life like food, music, sports, the beauty of nature and art.; easy going; tolerant, patient; always with mechanical equipment as in carpentry,

decorating graphic art, fashion, cooking or any work
demanding attention to detail.

Extraverted Intuitive

 These are spontaneous, innovative, initiating, non-
conforming and versatile; identifies the practical
possibilities in a situation; quick, focus on entire situation,
flexible; enjoys complexity; adaptable and easy acquisition
of new skills.

Extraverted Feeling

They are warm, friendly, sensitive; value friendship; tactful,
try to meet other's needs; adhering to societal values and
appropriate behavior; valuing others opinions; wanting
approval; full of zest and enthusiasm; able to express
feelings freely; strong awareness of likes and dislikes;
harmonious, empathic.

Extraverted Thinking

These are very good at organizing and labeling facts into
logical units; supporting laws, objectives, policies and
rules; governed by reason and not emotion; striving for
perfection based on universal idea or law; judge behavior

on the ideal model; treat others fairly but impersonally; wanting to find meaning in life and the world; wanting to get things done with the least cost in time and energy and plan ahead.

INTROVERTS

Introverted Sensation
Awareness of bodily sensation, both physical and emotional; good with routine, non-distractible, persevering; good memory and recall; adhering to own inner sense of reality which may be at odds with others; strong aesthetic appreciation often for abstract forms of art.

Introverted Intuitive
Guided by own inner images, seldom limited for long to a single perspective; inner fantasy life; May have difficulty communicating insights to others; good insight into complex situations; uses metaphors to explore possibilities; creative, quick insight into relationships with others; often has innovative ideas with creative meanings.

Introverted Feeling

Using own internal standard to judge people and things, not submitting to peer pressure or current trends, loyal, devoted, knowing own likes and dislikes, Often Idealistic, working for a cause or purpose; may not be overtly affectionate, holding tenderness and passionate conviction in reserve; often believe they understand others but experience themselves as misunderstood; strong sense of values and ethics.

Introverted Thinking

Analyzing the world based on own inner conviction and abstract categories, not easily influenced by others; enjoying intellectual activities, abstract ideas, subjects like philosophy, math, crossword puzzles; decisive with ideas working from principles; unconcerned with practical application of their work; often work independently and may be shy with people.

Based on what you have learnt about yourself up to this point I suppose you can figure out which kind of personality you belong to referencing on the listed characteristics.

CHAPTER SEVEN
KNOWLEDGE, EXPOSURE AND INFORMATION

Knowledge means the facts, information and skills acquired through education or experience. In other words, it is that theoretical or practical understanding you have on a particular subject. This means that having knowledge about something gives you the ability to understand how things work and the more knowledgeable you are the more advantage you have over other people and still you are better equipped to manage yourself and others, something that makes your life journey easy.

As humans there are so many things we need to learn so as to be better people, things like; understanding our strengths and weaknesses, mastering techniques of adjusting and accommodating with changes in our environment and or life situation, maintaining healthy relationships with people, making best judgments and decisions that can push for success, knowing how to assert our views and respecting other people's good views but as you can see all those crucial aspects require knowledge.

You should entirely search for knowledge because it is one of the things that account to your success. It is domineering that you put that gift of knowledge to proper usage so as to attain feats and heights in every realm of life.

Once you acquire knowledge you cannot remain the same, as it comes with a very big impact for example it makes you superior especially when you possess special knowledge in a special domain. Below are some of the reasons why knowledge is important;

Knowledge is the fuel that drives human life, this means that knowledge prepares a person to live a long and successful life.

Secondly, it is knowledge that distinguishes human from animals. Man controls all creatures on earth because of the gift of knowledge God blessed him with that also helps him to differentiate between what is right and wrong hence making him superior over all the other creatures.

Knowledge also shapes our personality especially when it comes to perfecting our behavior and dealing with people from different walks of life, so knowledge is not only important in science and technology as you would think but even in personality development.

Knowing the importance of knowledge, people must look up to all potential avenues to gain knowledge and make good use of it. The great men in history who put their knowledge to proper use have reached dignified heights in that even after very many years past their deaths we still remember them on this earth, that is how much knowledge can bring you.

Exposure

Exposure in simple terms means awareness of something. In this case we shall take it that you have seen how different people do different things in life and the impacts they cause such that those things are no longer strange or new to you. Probably you might be wondering how exposure is important to this effect but no worries we shall get to that. I said earlier that living on earth we are not living in a vacuum; we are surrounded by various components of the environment which influence our personality as well as the life we live. It is at this point that I would like to emphasize that we should not take what we see around us for granted and develop a habit of seeking more knowledge about those usual things and situations we are exposed to in our daily life. As you continue to search for knowledge you get exposed to more aspects in life which at the end of the day will make you more knowledgeable and superior in some domains that probably people have hardly thought about. The reason why exposure is important as you plan to awaken your potential is that the more you get exposed to different spheres of life the more knowledgeable you become and the more knowledgeable you become the more successful you will be in your field of expertise.

Information

Information refers to the facts that have already acquired meaning and so they can be used in decision making on a particular issue at hand or taken as knowledge. Information is a very crucial aspect in life. In order to survive in life everyone needs information because it also forms the basis of most of the decisions we take as humans. We shall not discuss about information into much detail but all you need to note here is that all the three aspects mentioned in the chapter; knowledge, exposure and information are very critical and decisive in your life. Mastering those three aspects makes you a unique, superior, Knowledgeable, progressive and successful person. They actually open up your minds like we would say "thinking outside the box". Thinking outside the box means that you have an open mind that can easily adjust and accommodate with new ideas depending on the issue at hand.

Having relevant information and exposure on something adds onto your knowledge about something and once you are knowledgeable about a particular subject then you are in better position to understand and control it well because knowledge is power.

Do not take everything in life for granted but in steady always take any available opportunity that can give you exposure, more information and knowledge because the more information, exposure and knowledge you get the better you become personally in the significant areas of life like decision making where you will be able to take informed decisions that promote your goals, maintaining positive attitude among others. The three are key elements you must consider as you plan to awaken your potential make sure you are always upbeat with those three components of life by seeking more of each in whatever you chose to do because they make you more knowledgeable, powerful and relevant in that field which eventually will make you a star in that field and own it followed by the attached benefits.

Just like knowledge, information is power. All informed people are not just mere people because they possess valuable data and information in them so they are highly respected that is why I want to encourage you to access as much information as you can without getting tired. Never block any channel from which you can get any kind of information that may be relevant to you now or later. It is very reliving to be an informed person rather than being an emergency hunter for information. *Emergency hunters for information* are those people who only seek and search for information when there is a crisis, you don't have to be one of that kind to wait for a crisis before you take the information to be serious. It is important that you always take every piece of information you get valuable and relevant until proved otherwise. In 2020 the whole world was on tension because of Corona Virus which caused COVID-19 disease. It is said to have started from China in Wuhan city. It was indeed a very strange disease it spread so fast but before it spread to other parts of the world, people had already been informed about its existence in china and advised to take certain precautions for safety, unfortunately many people ignored the measures and when the virus broke into their borders it really ripped lots of lives and that is when everyone came to believe that the virus is real and now everyone was so eager to get information about the virus, at this point every information that they came across regarding corona virus was crucial to them regardless as to whether fake or factual they couldn't take any more chances. Therefore, if they hard valued the prior information and did as advised the infection rate would have been minimal in the whole world.

*"Value every piece of information
you receive until proved
otherwise."*

The more you seek information the more you become
exposed and knowledgeable about that subject hence
becoming relevant and influential in that field. If you want
to fully awaken your potential, it is imperative that you
make the three elements of Knowledge, exposure and
information part of you entirely.

There are a number of things you can do to help you
acquire more knowledge, exposure and information for
which some of these include;

Making every bit of your movements purposeful. This can
be achieved by ensuring that you learn something new
each time you move. This however calls for your attention
during such movements such that you are able to identify
any new aspects that you can augment into your life to
create a difference.

Work on your reading culture. Many people avoid reading
actually they hate reading books but reading is very

healthy and informative. It exposes you to so many things like real life experiences, discoveries, social help, among others, from victims who decide to share such experiences through writing books. Several books are available that can enlighten you on different things in life and equip you with information that can change your life forever. Such books have the power to change your attitude towards life so when you finish reading this book make it a habit to read more bestselling books especially the ones categorized as self-help books.

Engaging in positive discussions with other people. This is because people have different levels of exposure, knowledge and information so as you discuss with them you get to know many new ideas and information which further opens your mind and introduces you to other people's thinking and knowledge about a similar subject.

Keep informed on what is trending, you must always keep track of what is trending all the time to get exposed, keep seeking knowledge and information because these are powerful weapons when it comes to personal development. Do not allow to be left behind in any of those three complementary aspects or else your efforts will be as good as nothing.

"keep seeking information, knowledge and exposure as long as you leave because they make you a special agent in a particular field you chose to operate in."

CHAPTER EIGHT
POSITIVE THINKING

Did you know that a weak mind is a devil's workshop too? A weak mind is one that is always idle and comfortable in that state. A weak and idle mind share a bunch of characteristics like laziness, negativity and poor thinking among others. I sometimes think that such people's minds are flipped because what is generally perceived positive in real life to them it is negative and then what normal minds generally consider abnormal to them it is nothing. Such people may need a hand of God to open their eyes before they can see the proper picture of life.

I will now twist this a little because now you are thinking that a weak mind is one that doesn't think straight, lazy to work and idle etc. but this is not true, that is not what I mean. In this sense the weak mind is that kind of mind that is scared of taking on challenges that can eventually change and or improve their wellbeing. It is said that one of the richest parts of the world is soil simply because of the multibillion ideas buried with people in their brains but I want also to add that the world is the poorest because people are intentionally mean with their multibillion ideas which can be transformed into multibillion projects. However, on the other hand the big enemy who has ensured that people remain with such big projects in their head is called _weak mind._

Many times, people develop brilliant ideas in their minds, ideas that actually can be developed into multimillion projects but because of the effect of having a weak mind, such ideas are locked up inside their brains forever. I know you too have ever developed a brilliant idea that could make you rich and or influential in life but you have turned yourself down, convincing yourself that maybe you don't have what it takes, no capital, no skills, poor government policies, no space, no time etc. yet still you have seen others who have started small in their businesses and grown into big stores and businesses within the same situation you are complaining about. The problem is not actually those issues above but your weak mind, you are just scared of that challenge. I tell you that even if those issues are settled you will not start because you will begin worrying about its future and worries will never end simply because you are scared to take up a challenge. A weak mind lacks self-discipline that is why they lack the element of determination.

Failure to put forth any ideas from your head to play is a clear manifestation of a weak mind you possess which you must get rid of. A weak mind actually beats odds in that it doesn't matter whether you are knowledgeable, wise, hardworking, informed, exposed etc. for as long as you are scared or incapable of bringing out what is inside you like rolling out a brilliant idea into reality, your mind is weak and you can never progress because you will have limited your own potential.

Below are some of the common aspects relating to people with weak minds.

Fear for failure. People with weak minds are static and always in comfort zone not because they are lazy to work or that they have achieved their goals but simply because *they are scared of failure* in case they venture into new challenges.

Compromise. People with weak minds in most cases have very good ideas to themselves which surely if executed they can change their lives forever but they compromise such ideas due to the fear for failure which stops them from trying out such ideas practically.

Fear for personal accountability. The weak-minded people always have good ambitions and ready to work harder to achieve them but they worry about being accountable for their own failure so they end up opting for the comfort they are enjoying apparently rather than pushing their ideas to reality.

They are feeble. They easily give up and can hardly get along with progressive people who keep trying out new things because they think that such people are not cautious enough, they will completely crash.

Generally looking at the kind of people they are based on the aspects mentioned above, it shows that weak minded people are actually very potential people in life but their only problem is fear. They are so scared of failure and there is no way you can progress once you are controlled by fear. They say cowards live longer but the truth is that they achieve very little compared to the longer time they live and when they die, they die with a lot of brilliant ideas in them. That is why I also agree that someone's death is not a tragedy but what dies inside them is the real tragedy because you can never know how much impact it would bring about in people's lives.

That is exactly how bad a weak mind limits your capability and makes you believe that your current situation is the best and final because it blocks you from thinking ahead. However, the good news is that you can easily transform the weak mind into a strong mind by only breaking the tie with fear for challenges and then develop a strong forward looking, creative, ambitious and flexible mind that thinks positively.

A strong mind is also called a positive mind and it is the right mind set that we ought to possess if we are to succeed in life.
Having a positive mind is very beneficial in a number of ways some of which include;

A positive mind is always working to improve and move to higher levels. Such a mindset is always ready to face any kind of challenge that comes its way and very determined to try out new things including testing their ideas on ground; such people look at failure as a mere alert that they have started a new thing which they have to accomplish but not a threat.

People with positive minds are all the time busy thinking forward on how to make tomorrow better than today rather than wasting time on useless things. Such people are the masters of positive thinking, they never give up just like that nor scared of starting up something new like putting out their ideas from the head to the ground to see what happens with it, in case they fail they call it a lesson and indeed they learn from their failures and mistakes.

Thinking positive encourages you to work harder since you constantly desire to move to higher levels.

Positive thinking helps you to get rid of laziness and idleness because it makes you creative and ambitious hence keeping you busy all the time.

Positive thinking also helps you maintain self-discipline it is always presenting to you new challenges and ideas to think about and manage.

Positive thinking also helps you build and maintain a positive attitude which encourages you to go ahead and achieve your goals.

Thinking positive means having a positive attitude and flexible to situations without losing morale and hoping for the best in everything you do. This kind of attitude keeps you going and achieving your goals as well as enabling you to practice your creativity and explore new ideas. Since a positive mind is not scared of failure, it also helps you develop a free and flexible mind. Therefore, in order to fully awaken and exploit your potential you need to build and maintain the aspect of positive thinking because it puts you in a better position by making you think straight and target the end regardless even when you detect failure you just keep hope ahead of you. Strong minds never give up and failures are just reminders that they have started a journey.

"Winners are not those who never fail
but those who never give"

I would like to encourage you to embrace positive thinking in your life which will help you to unlock and utilize your potential in the most effective way. This I mean that you must be more creative, determined, forward looking and above all keep your trust in God because he is the master planner.

Once you have a positive mind and you are thinking positively, failures and weaknesses cannot bring you down but instead they will act as lessons in life to add on your knowledge and experience for which experience is the best teacher. This will drive you towards achieving your goals.

"A weak-minded person is someone
who is scared of bringing out the ideas in their mind
to play due to fear of failure."

A weak-minded person is a very good example of a failure.

CHAPTER NINE
HARD WORK

Does it necessarily mean that using a lot of physical energy to get something done is hard work? No. hard work is not all about physical energy but instead attitude towards work. Hard work is all about attitude and mental effort strictly. So, I would say that hardworking basically means keeping a positive attitude towards work regardless. You cannot determine how hardworking a person is by merely looking at how much physical energy they put in. There are a series of aspects that you can consider to identify or determine a hard-working person.

Scenario:

> Two farmers were hired to clear a hectare of land each for cultivation. The two men were expected to finish the work within a week working from 6:00am – 6:00pm each day.
> Farmer A finished the work in two days and Farmer B finished his work in four days.

Who of the two men is very hard working? I bet you'll go for gentleman A who finished within two days because you feel like he did a lot of work yet both cleared a hectare each but anyhow here is the point, the difference you have noticed in the time taken to finish the job by each farmer cannot determine who is hardworking though it may determine who is stronger.

Scenario 2:

In a big company usually the top managers' work like signing documents and chairing meetings, monitoring etc. requires less physical energy compared to the employees who load and offload cargo in the same company.

In this case if it is physical energy put in that determines a hardworking person, then the people who load and offload cargo take the praise actually but that is not the case. The managers are paid more because of their mental effort they put in to ensure that all the business functions are working well and that everyone is on board, again direct physical energy doesn't determine.

The two scenarios show that to be considered hard working is not about putting in much physical energy but there are other aspects considered to determine if really someone is hard working or not.

I have come up with a list of some aspects that I think can provide a fair yard stick to determine a hardworking person. You can also use them to determine whether you are hardworking or not;

Perseverance: This is one of the parameters that can be used to determine someone's attitude towards work which eventually shows whether one is hard working or not. Perseverance means that you accept to work positively even when the conditions are hush and unfavorable. Usually people who persevere and continue to work with the same attitude even when working conditions change to the worst are fit to be considered hard working otherwise if not then their attitude will drop and they stop performing if they are not mentally strong (hard working).

Persistence: This is another parameter that can be considered to identify hard working people at work places.

People who are hardworking are always persistent in whatever they do. Persistence is where you keep going, keeping a positive attitude and never giving up because your focus is at the end. No matter what challenges come your way you are not moved you maintain your positive attitude at work hoping for the best later. That is being hard working.

Determination and commitment: Some one's determination and commitment mean a lot towards maintaining a positive attitude towards work. Usually people who are determined are actually committed to work they ignore all the other factors that my destruct them and focus on the main goal for which they are working to achieve. Determined and committed people are always hard working. Non hardworking people are never determined nor committed that is why they give up so easily and get lazy to work when conditions change regardless of whether they are strong or weak.

Ability to learn from situations: Hard work can also be determined from your ability to learn from the prevailing situations at the work place as well as adapting to the changes in the working environment. In most cases hardworking people take keen interest to quickly learn new things that can improve on their personality and skills. This is not the case with non-hardworking people because for them sometimes you may have to force them to learn new skills.

Sacrifice: This parameter is a little unique and may not surely be so evident but the hardworking people can easily exhibit this aspect especially through the amount of time they spent doing company work after normal hours. They sacrifice their time for the company or at times they decide to offer extra services voluntarily when there is need.

Always give their best: Hardworking people always give their best towards work to a point that their presence and absence are equally felt. Therefore, hard work can be determined by looking at how much someone puts in at the work place.

All the parameters above are rational they can fairly be used to determine who a hard working person is, rather than thinking that the one who uses more physical energy is the most hard working.

 If you have to check your status as per hard working, check yourself alongside those parameters mentioned above and see where you belong, remember I told you that throughout this book you must be honest to yourself if you are to benefit. Each parameter counts and if your score is low please master those aspects very well and adopt them, make them part of you such that you can become a hard-working person whether you are self-employed or an employee elsewhere.

CHAPTER TEN
SHIFTING BLAME

In life we face so many challenges, many times we overcome or sometimes we fail. we know very well that failing is not the end of life perhaps it is just the beginning of life so it is a wrong mentality to let one failure define your life forever like some people do. Actually I don't encourage anyone to feel bad when they fail at some point just keep going it does not matter how many times you try and fail, it is that last time you try that is most important in your life because it will either push into success or into self-destruction if you don't believe in yourself.

"Never count how many times you try and fail but only count how many times you succeed."

There are so many things that contribute to our success and personal development right from childhood. All those elements that we credit to shape our personality in life are equally important since each influences our being in a unique way while complementing the other factors. However much as all those factors play in our favor when we control and manage them positively to shape our personality and determine our levels of success, the absolute power to succeed lives inside us, we determine our success levels in fact we are the limits to our own potential.

By the time we are born into this world each of us is blessed with a special talent or a special skill that can make you special in some way which is your number one asset and it is the potential inside you. Meanwhile merely having that talent inside you does not automatically make you what you are supposed to be, there are a number of things like principles of life which you must adopt as part of your life such that they can help you to awaken that potential in you. All the aspects we have discussed in the various chapters of this book up to this point are almost all you need to apprehend in life to be successful and also to leave a soft and easy life.

But of course, like I mentioned earlier the power to decide on what kind of life we live is in us, take this from me that we decide our own life, success and failure. Therefore, it is not sensible enough for any one to blame someone else for their own failure. Each time you fail to succeed in anything cancel out that big option that many people embrace of blaming other parties for that registered failure. Some people totally become lazy to fight for their lives simply because they find comfort in blaming other parties when they fail. Honestly who really expects that someone will love them and care for them more than they do for themselves? There is no one who understands your life more than you do and if you don't personally understand your life or know who you are, your life is in danger. The people who mostly shift their blame to others or other parties so that they can achieve a free mind and feel free from guilt of causing their own failure are people who don't even know who they are and the potential that is inside them.

This is a very common habit among people especially those who face challenges in life with a negative attitude thinking that life has to be smooth and running in their favor. We have already discussed about what kind of people don't understand that challenges and failure are part of life so they keep on avoiding challenges and failure but once caught up in a challenge and they fail, they will quickly look for who or what to blame for such a challenge even when no one forced them into it.

Shifting blame is a very bad habit in life, it is like cheating on your own life because you are totally responsible for your own life and all the decisions you take including their effects. Before people learn to acknowledge their own mistakes and work on them to improve, they cannot progress however much they work hard. Being true to yourself is very important, it helps to tackle your true weaknesses and improve on them, it helps to know your capability, areas of interest, your potential, etc. which are all capable of fine tuning your attitude and shaping your personality to an appropriate nature which can then drive you to achieving your specific goals.

People who keep shifting their blame to other parties don't realize how mean and dangerous they are to themselves because they can't change or think about improving their weaknesses after all they know how to cover their weaknesses and failure so they remain like that, they never learn from such challenges their goal is making sure that it is not their blame regardless, that is what makes them happy.

Honestly if you cannot acknowledge your own mistakes and failure and you keep on shifting blame to others it shows how much you hate yourself, how much you don't care about yourself, how much you are wasting your potential in life and how weak minded you are. Acknowledging our own mistakes is very crucial in life, the more we take full responsibility of our own mistakes and weaknesses the more we create avenues of learning from such mistakes and improving on our weaknesses for better which at the end of it all make us better people as we get relevant help from other people because they exactly understand who we are including areas where we need help.

All in all, you should fight hard to develop and maintain a strong mind, appositive mind that is always forward looking which can allow you to acknowledge your own mistakes and weaknesses then go ahead to turn the weaknesses into strengths and also learn from your own mistakes. The only way you can show how much you love yourself is by being true and honest to yourself otherwise when you chose to compromise with yourself especially on identifying your weaknesses it is more less a self-destruction mission.

People who know and understand who they are, are governed by self-discipline which directs them on choosing between right and wrong and understanding that they are 100% responsible for their own life so they have to be very keen. I find it a very good idea to keep on self-examining yourselves to see how you are progressing in life see what issues you have encountered, which mistakes you have made, which weaknesses you have developed and so on such that you can know which areas you need to improve otherwise shifting blame does not help anyone to improve.

I have also realized how this awful behavior of shifting blame has blemished the youth in my country by giving them an excuse to spend all their time sleeping, playing stupid local games all day and drinking cheap dangerous alcohol among others without sparing even a second to think about their lives simply because the government has failed to create for them jobs. Is that real? Honestly who has ever been promised a job by the government? This is where they go wrong the government is not mandated to offer you a job but to create avenues through which people can find and get or create jobs. This means that it is your responsibility to explore those avenues and find a job or create a job for yourself. With that kind of attitude and self-deceit that the government is supposed to give them jobs they have become so lazy to explore the potential in themselves simply because they have someone to blame for their not having a job, this is insane and being myopic, okay then how has the government stopped them from fully achieving something from their natural talents and special skills that they possess or even their physical energy? These guys just don't want to work and now that the politicians like it when they are in such situations for easy manipulation, they continue to blind fold them and make them believe that it is the government responsible for their suffering and lack of jobs but is that right? How many have come together to join their skills, talents and so on to come up with something like a business? All they do is sit argue about wealthy artists and sports men plus politics in which they don't even understand a thing yet there is a lot that they can do in that time they waste. These youths have turned themselves stupid simply because they were relieved of the total responsibility of their actions in life by creating for them a shock absorber in the name of government which is held accountable instead. Just imagine if everyone stood up and directly assured those hopeless youths that they are fully responsible for their own life and they are to blame for the kind of lives they are living simply because they have not probably done enough to exploit their full potential to support themselves. This would be a hard-fair statement however right now it quite complicated because they are already wasted and convinced that the government is responsible to care for their lives and they should only wait to receive the jobs and work to do directly from the government to them.

It is a very complex attempt to try and drive such attitude from these youths at once just because they are now wasted, brain washed, hopeless, developed poor attitude, lost self-discipline, weakened minds, negative thinking etc.

you may see that they have lost control over their lives so the most effective attempt to start with if we are to change their mindset is pushing them into rehabilitation and help them understand who they actually are and their potential as humans then begin to create and develop a proper mindset in them stressing aspects of self-discipline, positive attitude, positive thinking, hard work, understanding people, and imparting necessary knowledge in them. This is what will help to change the attitude of our fellow youths who are completely wasted after being fooled to believe that the government owns their life so it has to do for them everything.

I am always disappointed when I see strong youths running up and down like house flies following every politician who passes in their area shouting, drunk with alcohol and drugs sponsored by the foolish politicians who take advantage of them during election periods. That is not being idle but lack of purpose in life and loss of control over one's own life.

With the kind of attitude, the youths are having right now, none of them can succeed even if everything needed is provided because they have developed a wrong mindset, attitude and wrong personality different from what they actually ought to be. The solution is helping them start new life by making them understand that they are totally accountable for whatever happens in their life and that no one can care about them more that they care for their lives and that no one will extract from them their full potential if they don't bring it out themselves. They must understand that it is all about them, success lies in their hands so they should explore more to identify their talents, special skills and areas of interest in which they can perform best and this will help them to build a whole new life around them as they explore their newly unleashed potential.

You may also be having some cases where you have found comfort in transferring blame to other parties it may not necessarily be a person but other things like tools, time, skills, whether etc. You must teach yourself to acknowledge all mistakes and weaknesses you possess once they are exposed. There is nothing that happens in your life without your knowledge the only problem is how we prioritize our activities. For example, missing a client at office when you reach late then you try to excuse yourself with traffic jam or sometimes rain, is it true that you have never thought that those two things can affect you someday? What plan did you put in place to encounter that? This means the problem is your poor planning not the rain or the traffic jam so in this case you are trying to shift blame and this can become part of you after all you have an excuse to give rather than putting a plan in place to overcome that challenge.

All in all, you must cutout the option of finding excuses when you make a mistake or do something wrong learn to acknowledge your mistakes, weaknesses and failures then learn from them to make yourself better and always keep a positive attitude and practice self-control all the time. Of course I don't guarantee that all the decisions, reactions and actions you take will be 100% perfect though it should be your benchmark but in case you realize it was your reaction or action or decision that caused the trouble be true to yourself and genuinely accept your mistake or failure in good faith don't dare find an excuse to justify your mistake or failure just correct it and or learn from it such that next time you are better at it. It is of no use to look smart over your fault by shifting the blame to another person, fine you may gain a free mind because you have managed to deny responsibility but what difference does it bring to your life? Stop fancying things that don't add value to you. I compare this kind of success to scoring in your own goal post when playing soccer.

I want you to look back during your free time and consider any past event or challenge where you had to shift blame for some reasons to another party yet in actual sense it was you to blame and see what you had to do rather than shifting blame. Please note that shifting blame doesn't only apply to people, it could be anything else. That is why we have heard people many times giving excuses like; I was let down by time, my boot messed me up at the pitch otherwise I should have scored that goal, etc. that is all nonsense the point is poor preparations.

> *"Shifting blame to other parties*
> *is one way of showing how much*
> *you hate yourself."*
> *Mubezi Arthur*